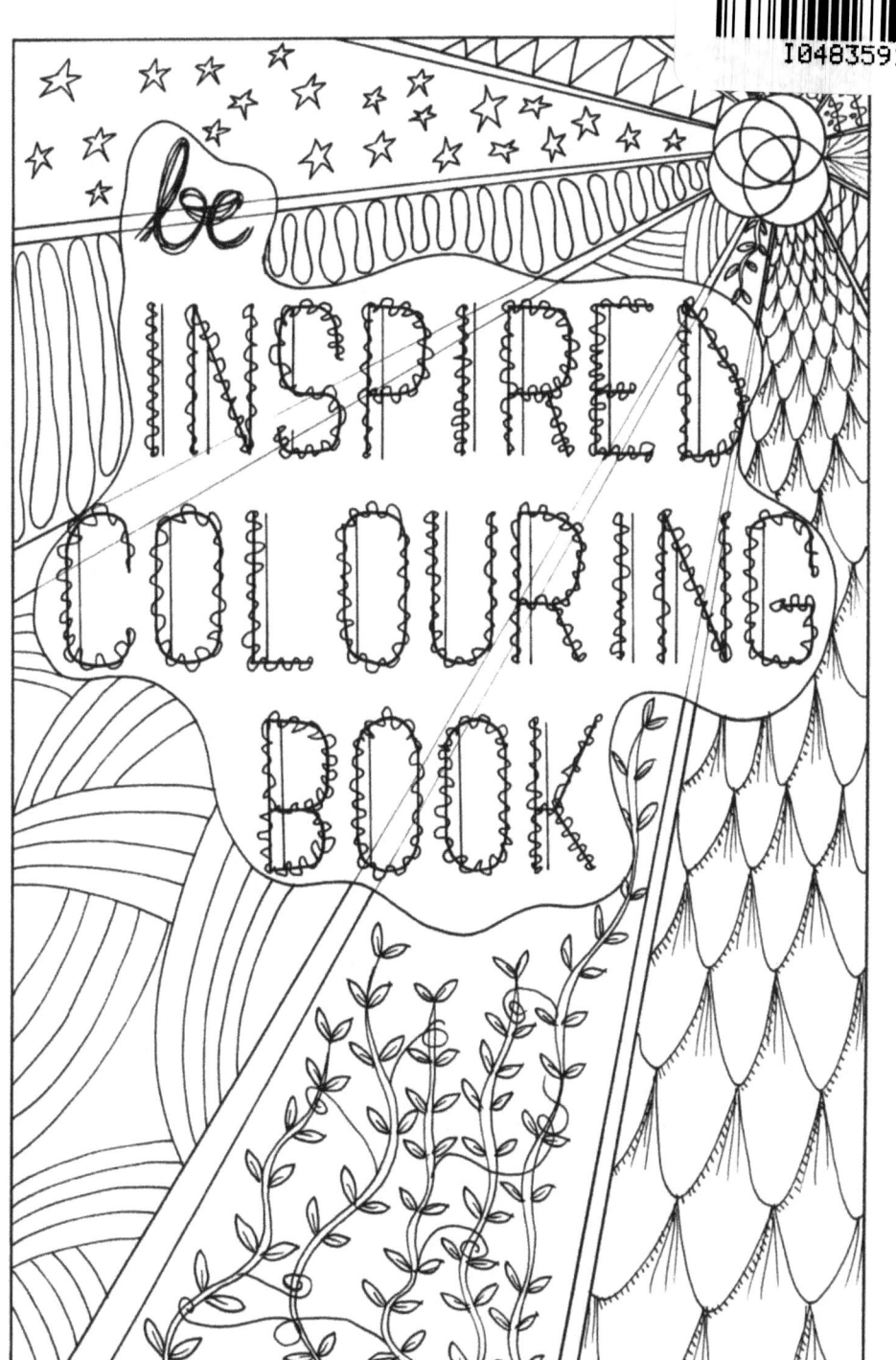

be INSPIRED COLOURING BOOK

Designs created by Katy Hollway
and coloured by

SozoPrint
SozoPrint.com

ISBN 978-0-9929404-8-5

Connect with the author at
www.katyhollway.com
www.facebook.com/KatyHollwayAuthor/
www.katyhollwayauthor.wordpress.com

Be Inspired Colouring Book

The following pages have been created for you to colour.
There are no restrictions to what palette you choose.

Beautiful images can be produced using similar,
complementary or contrasting colours.
Your palette could be motivated by nature, your favourite
shades or environment.

Each design is inspired by a word and will hopefully
inspire you.
As you colour, perhaps the word or design will trigger
some thoughts. These may be quotes from films or books.
Maybe they will provoke dreams and memories.
You could use the opposite page to collect your musings.

The designs are a mixture of simple and complicated
images.
You can colour the designs as they are or add further
patterns with a fine black pen.

The first part of the book is full of portrait orientated
images and is followed by landscape designs.

The book has been arranged so that, if you wish, your
completed designs can be framed and displayed without
removing other designs from the book.

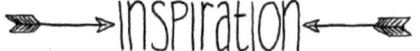

inspiration

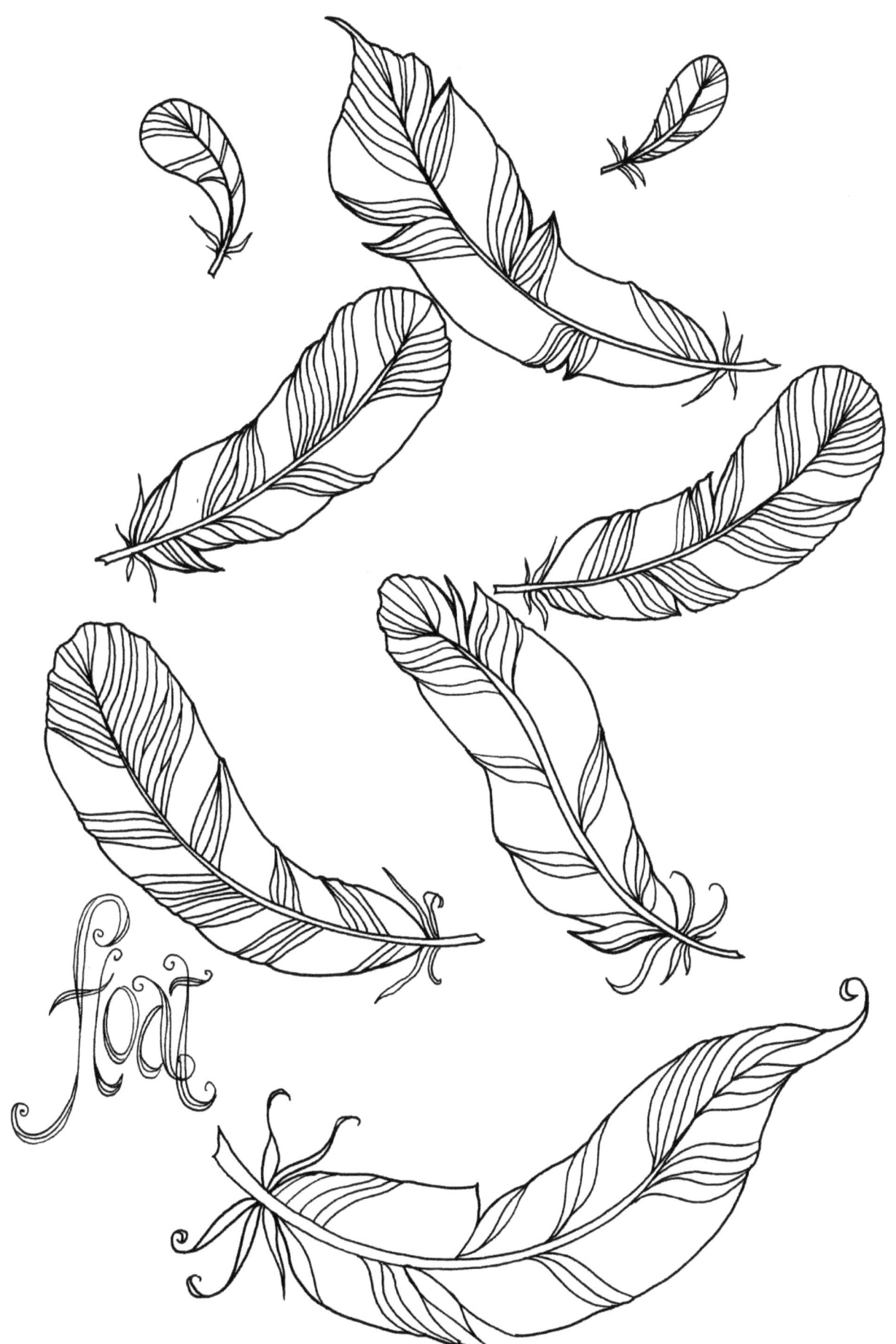

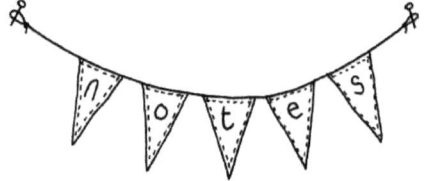

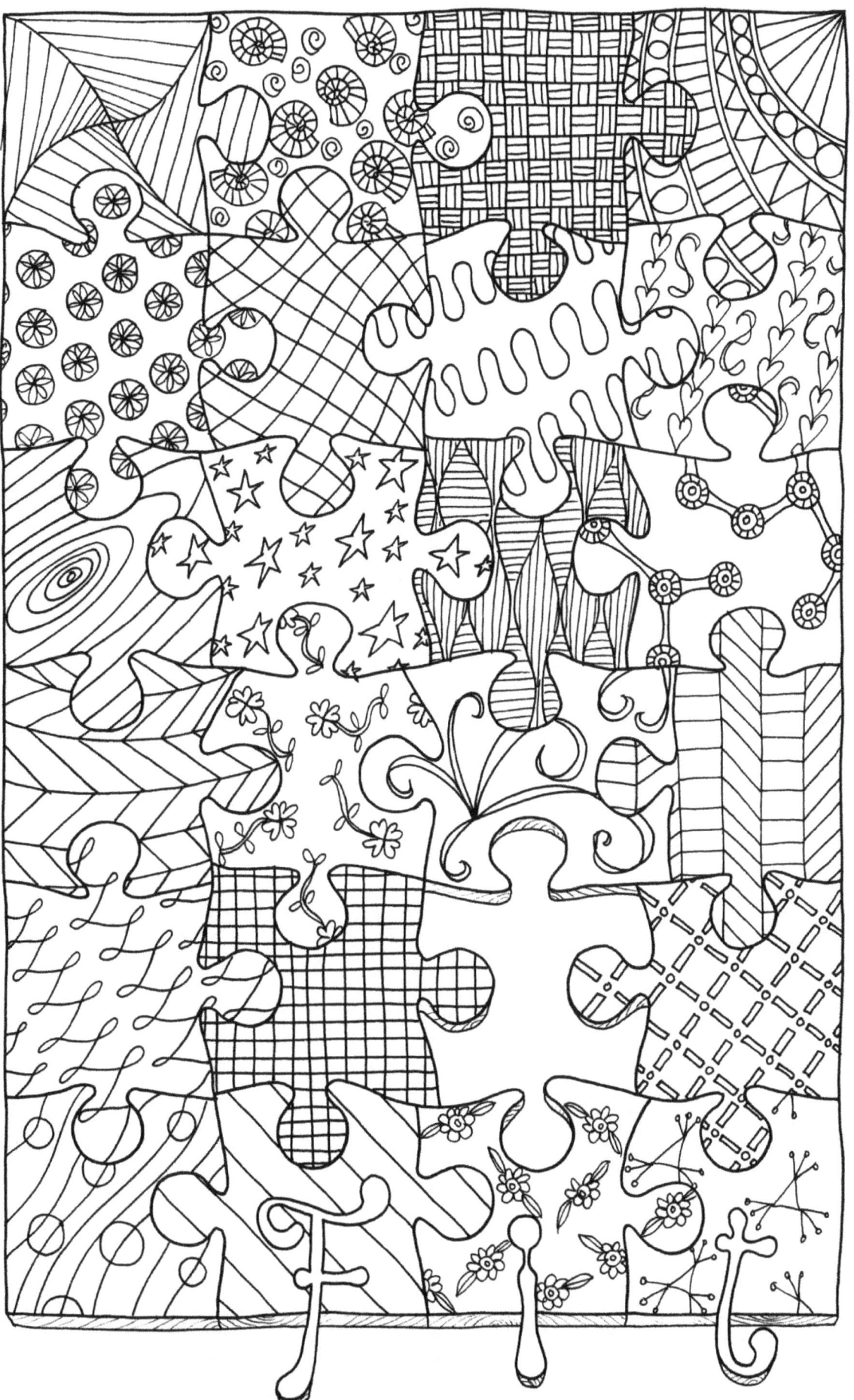

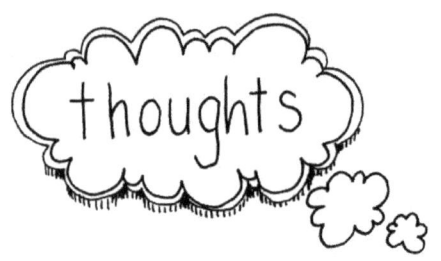

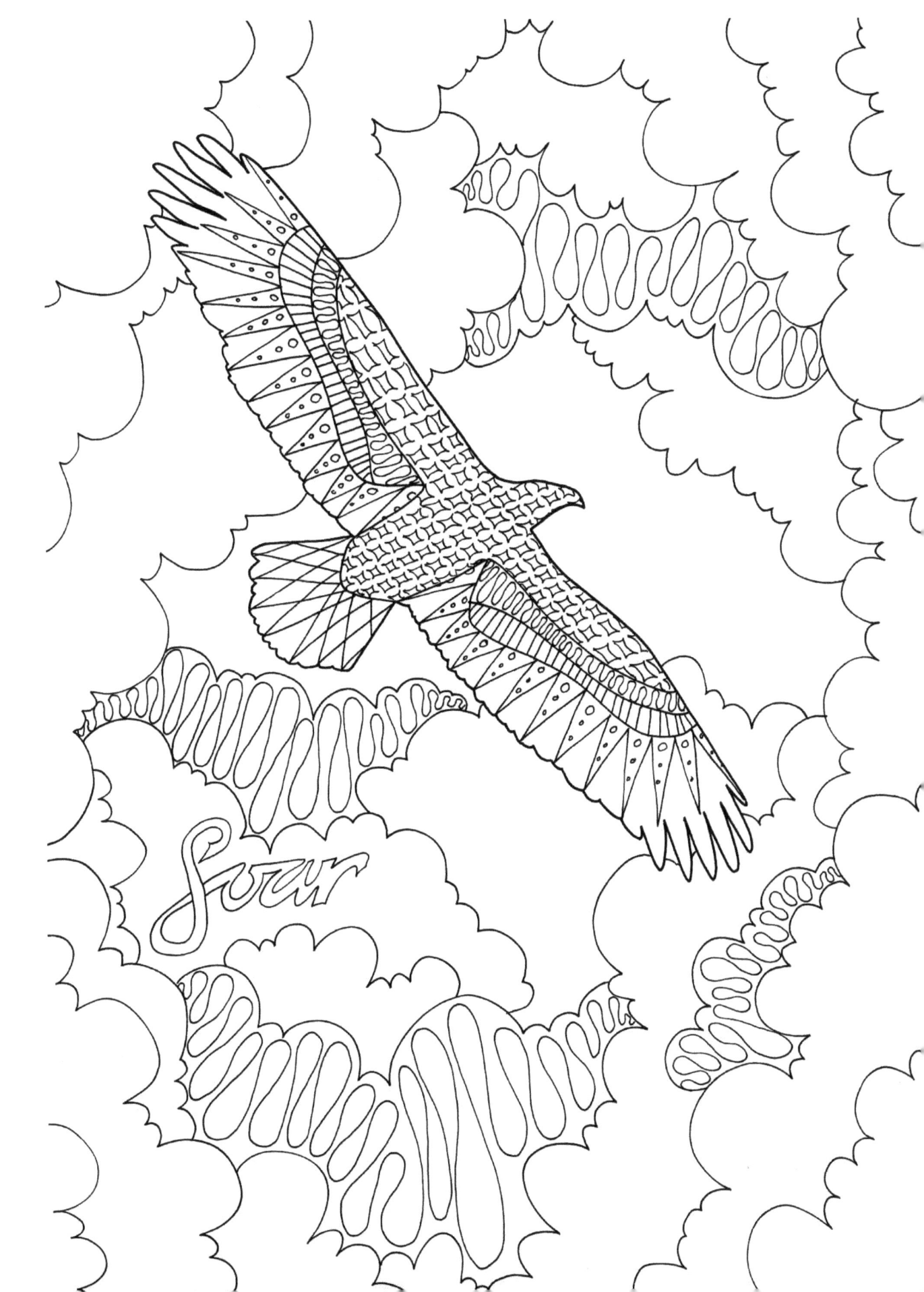

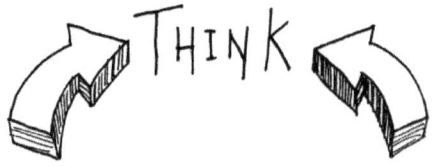

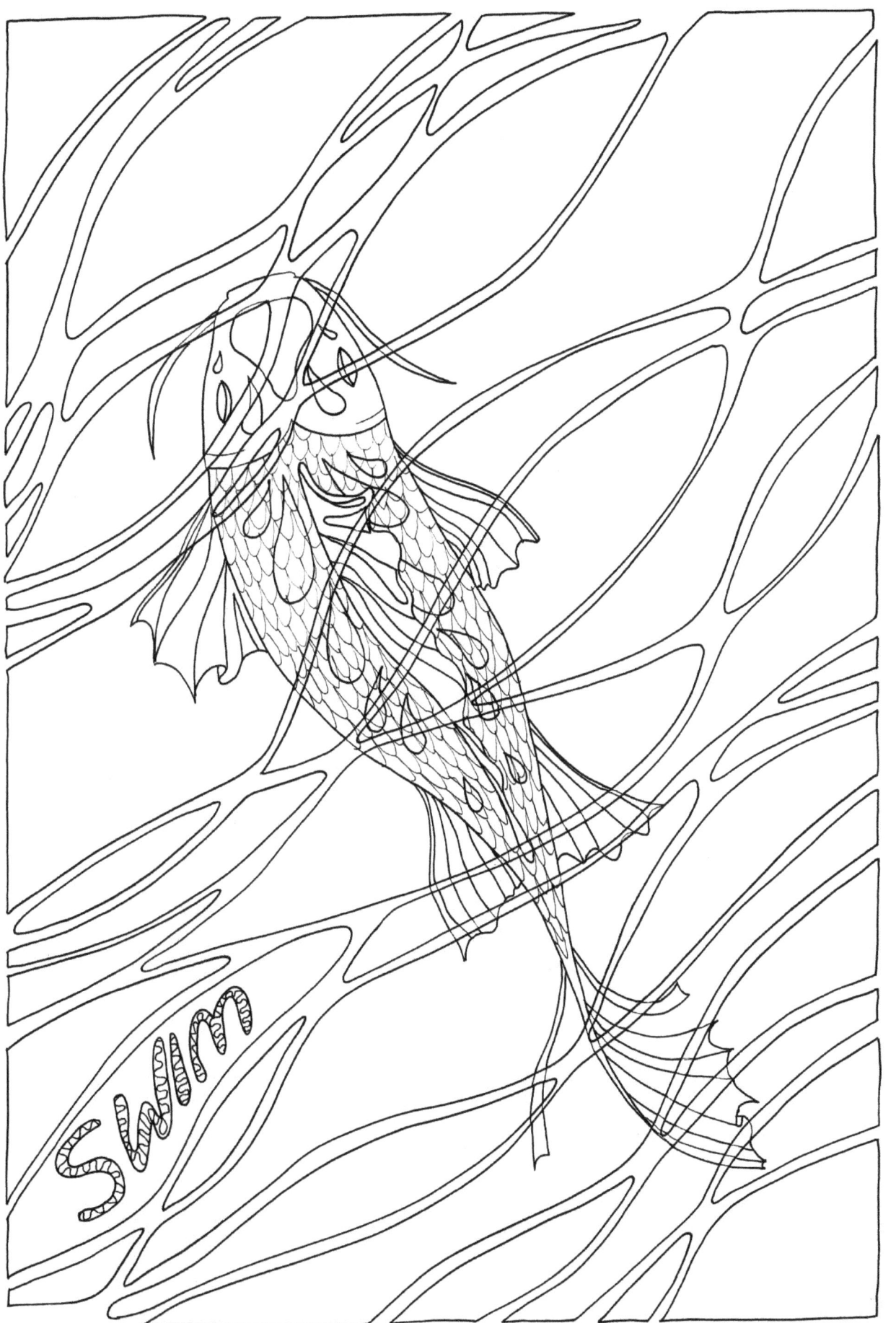

notes

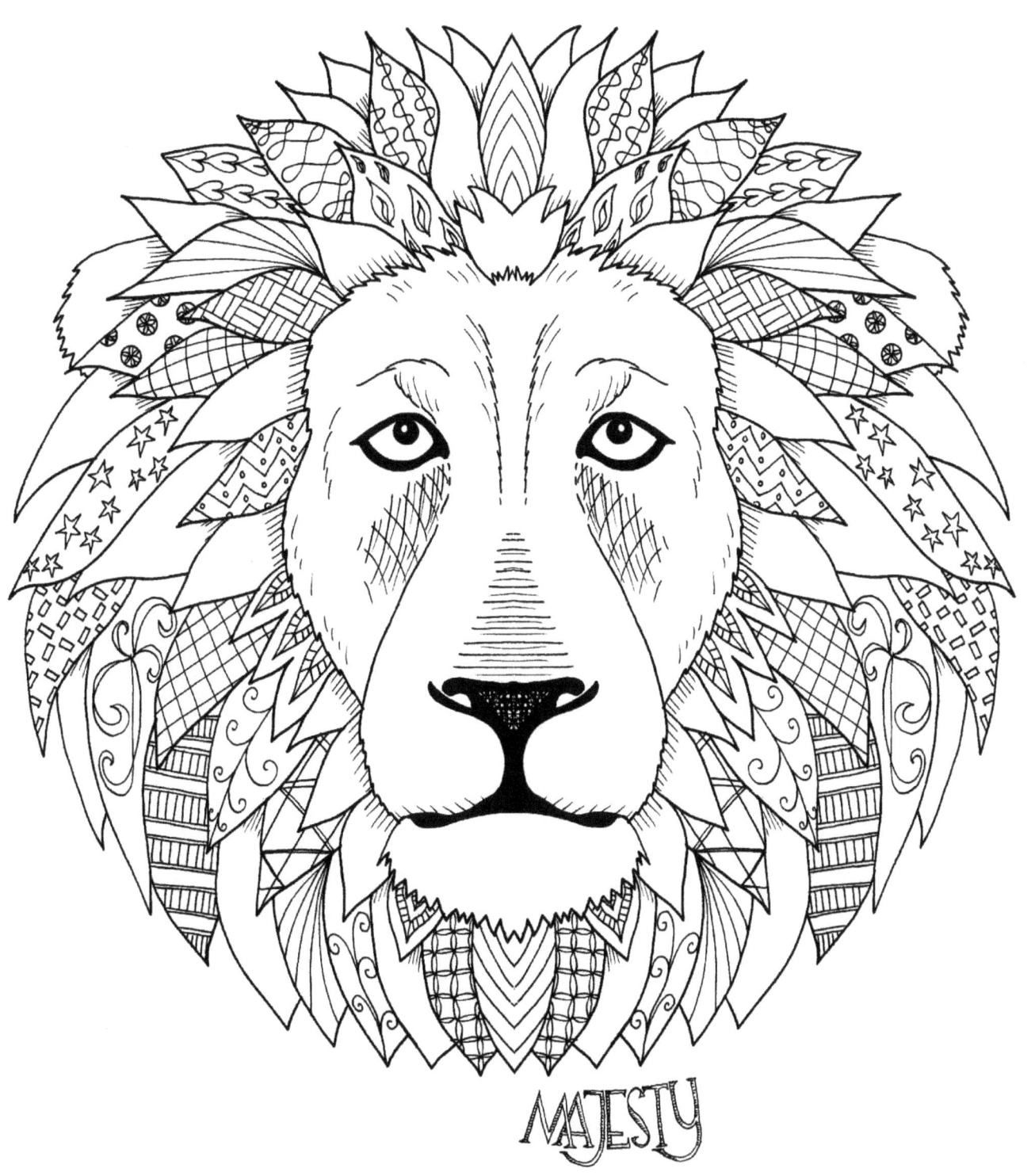

MAJESTY

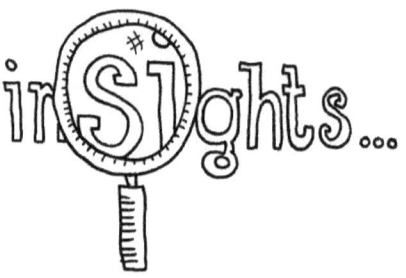

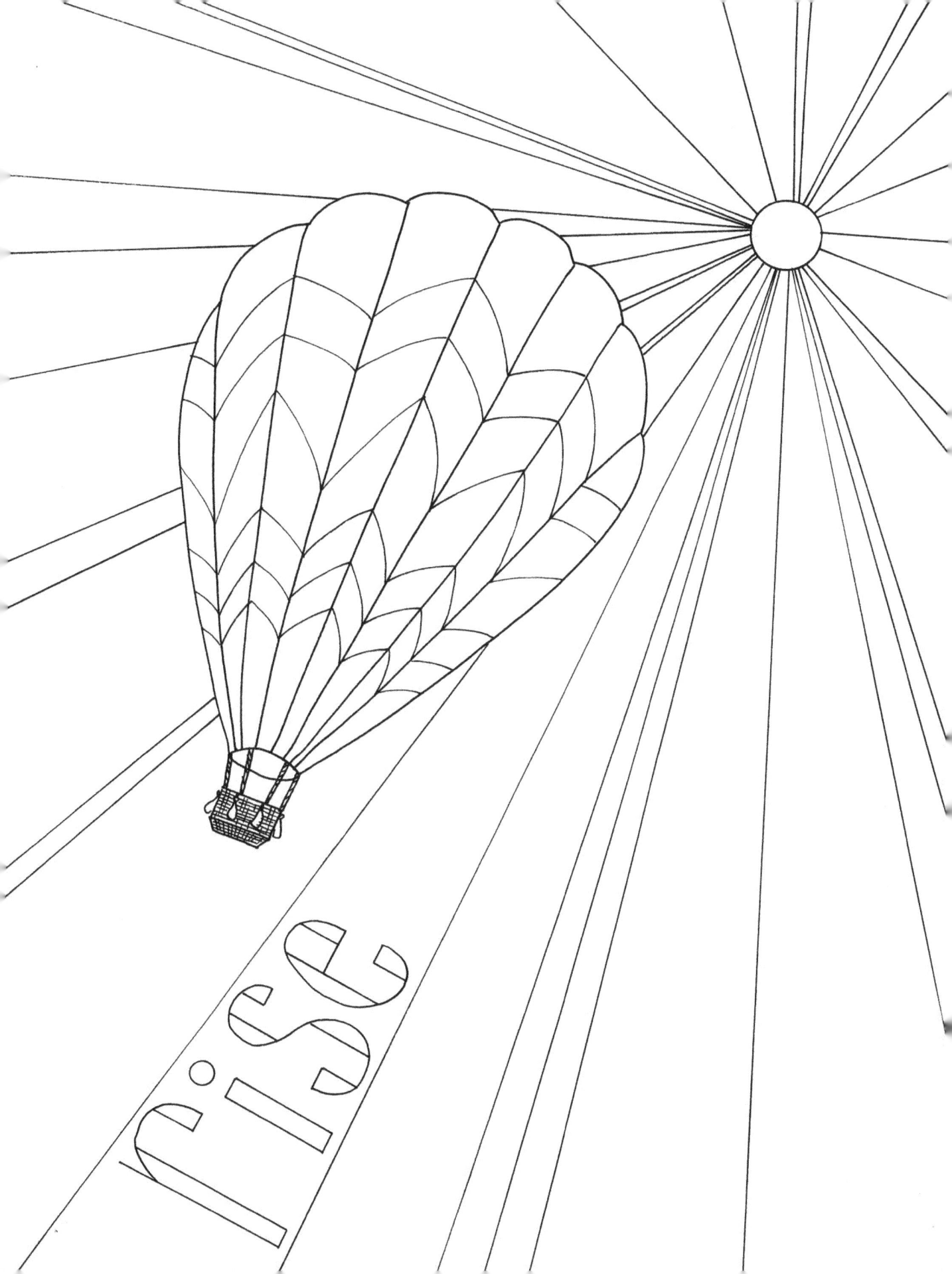

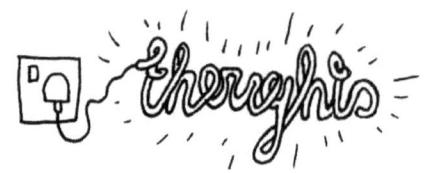

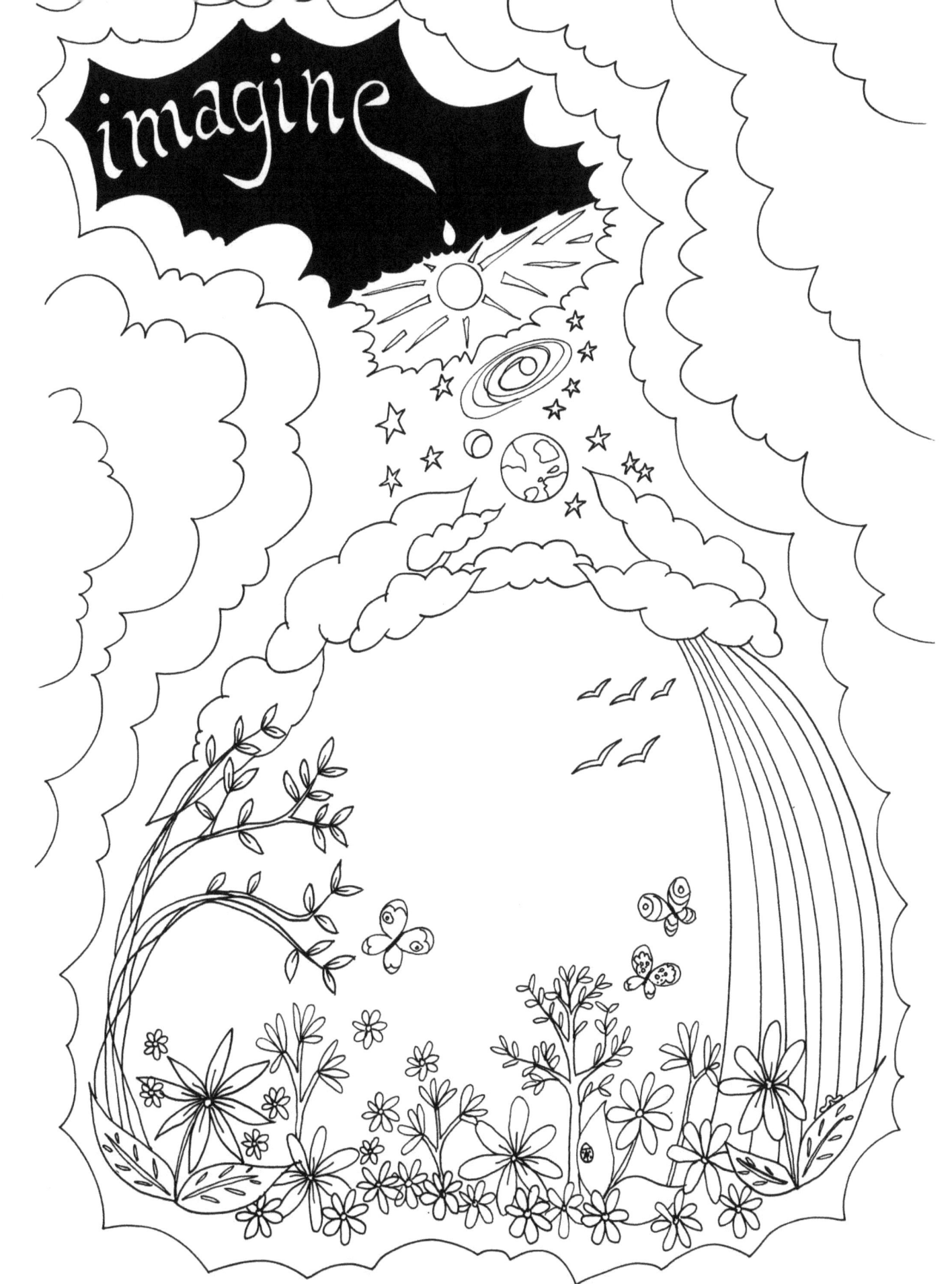

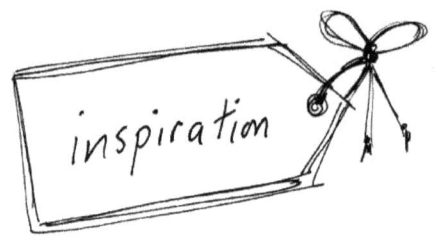

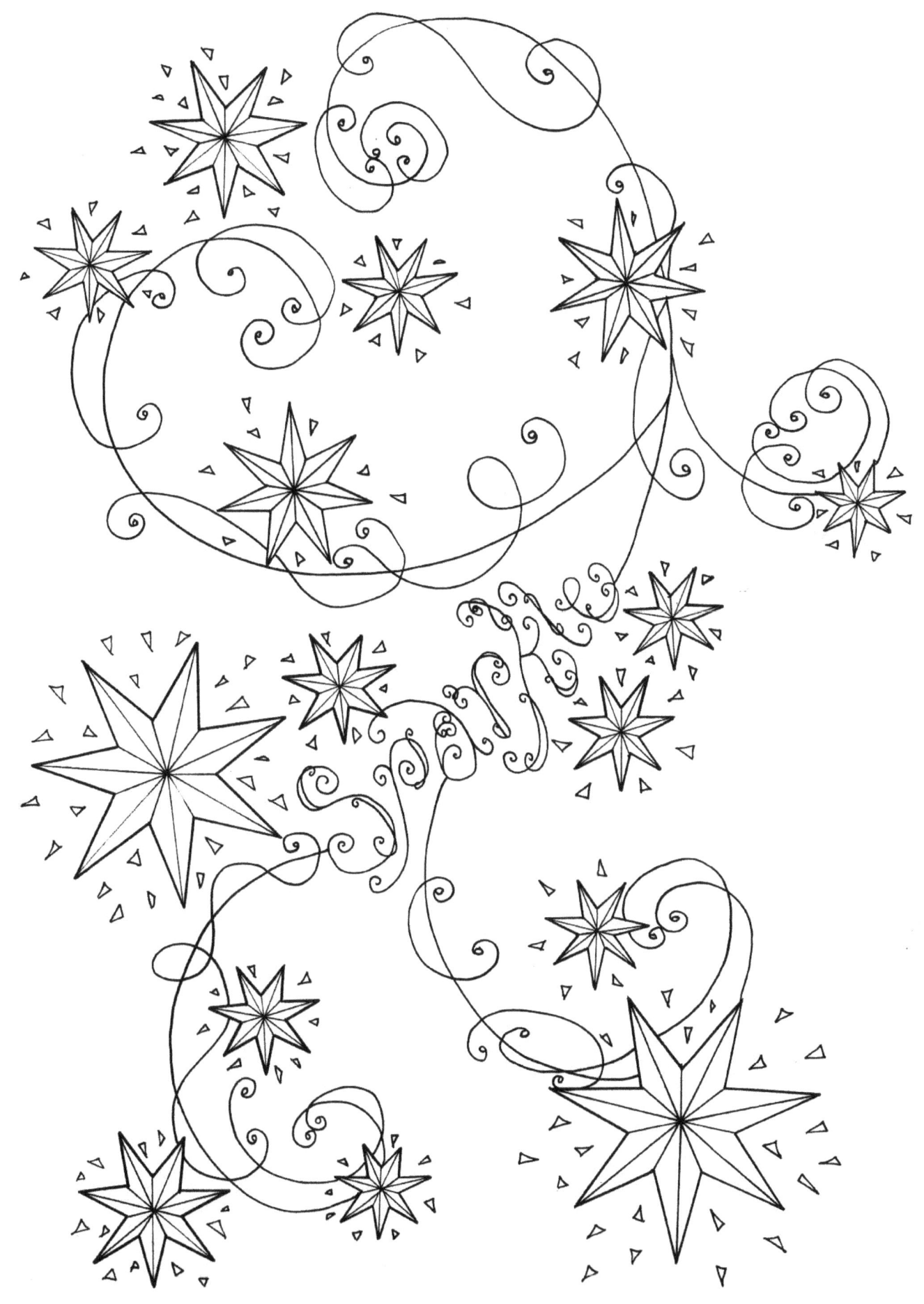

inspiration

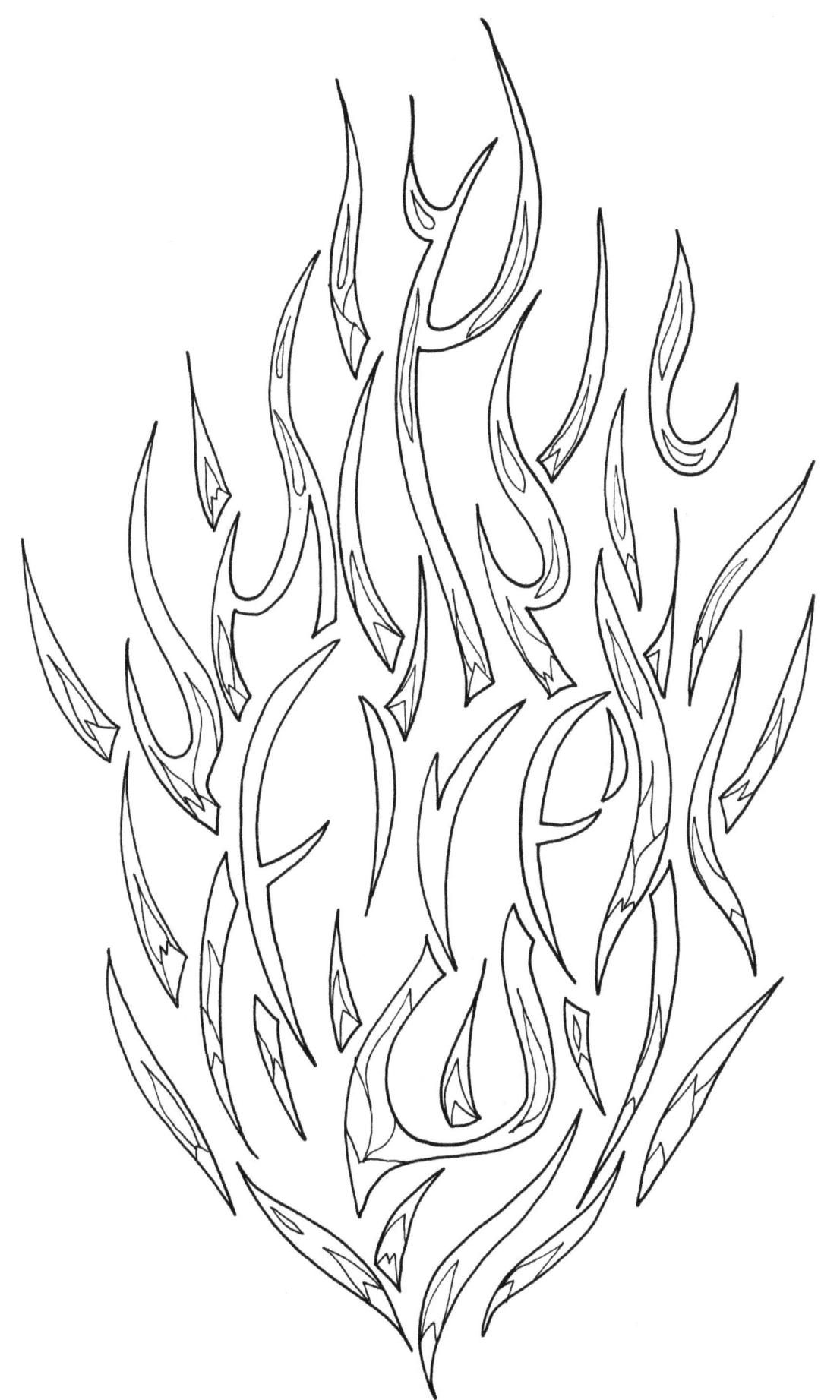

thoughts

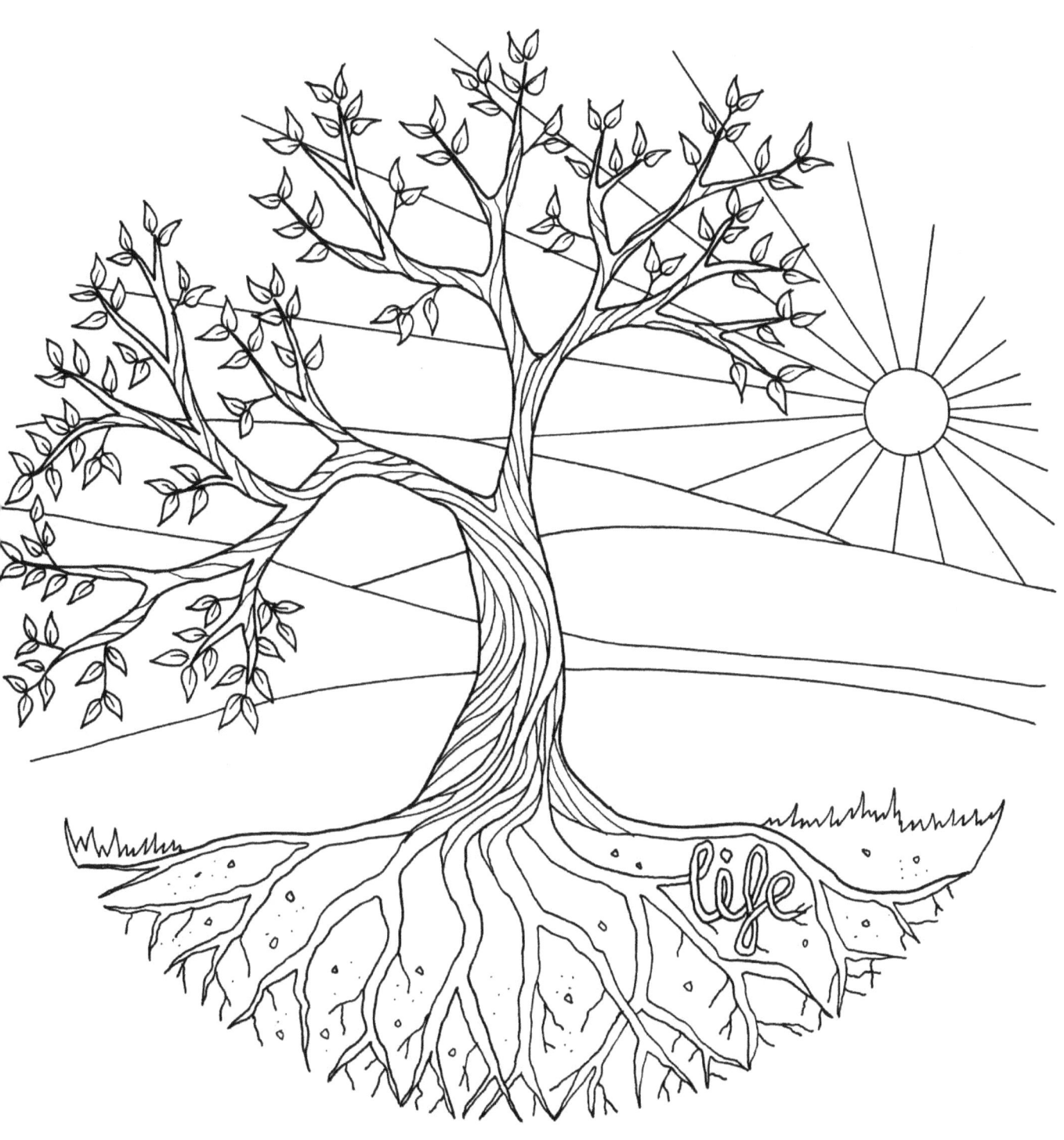

thoughts

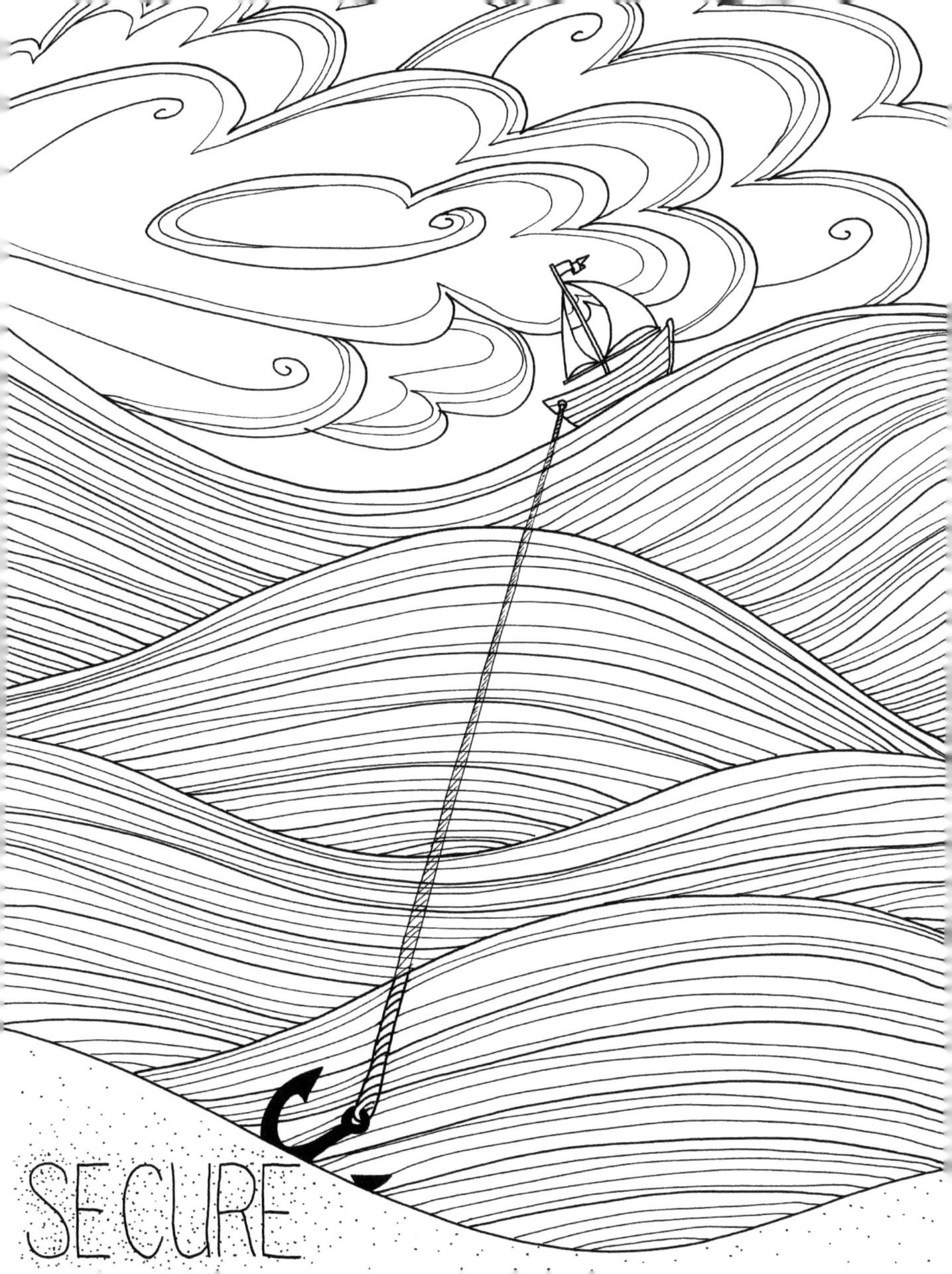

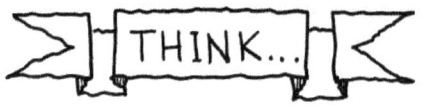

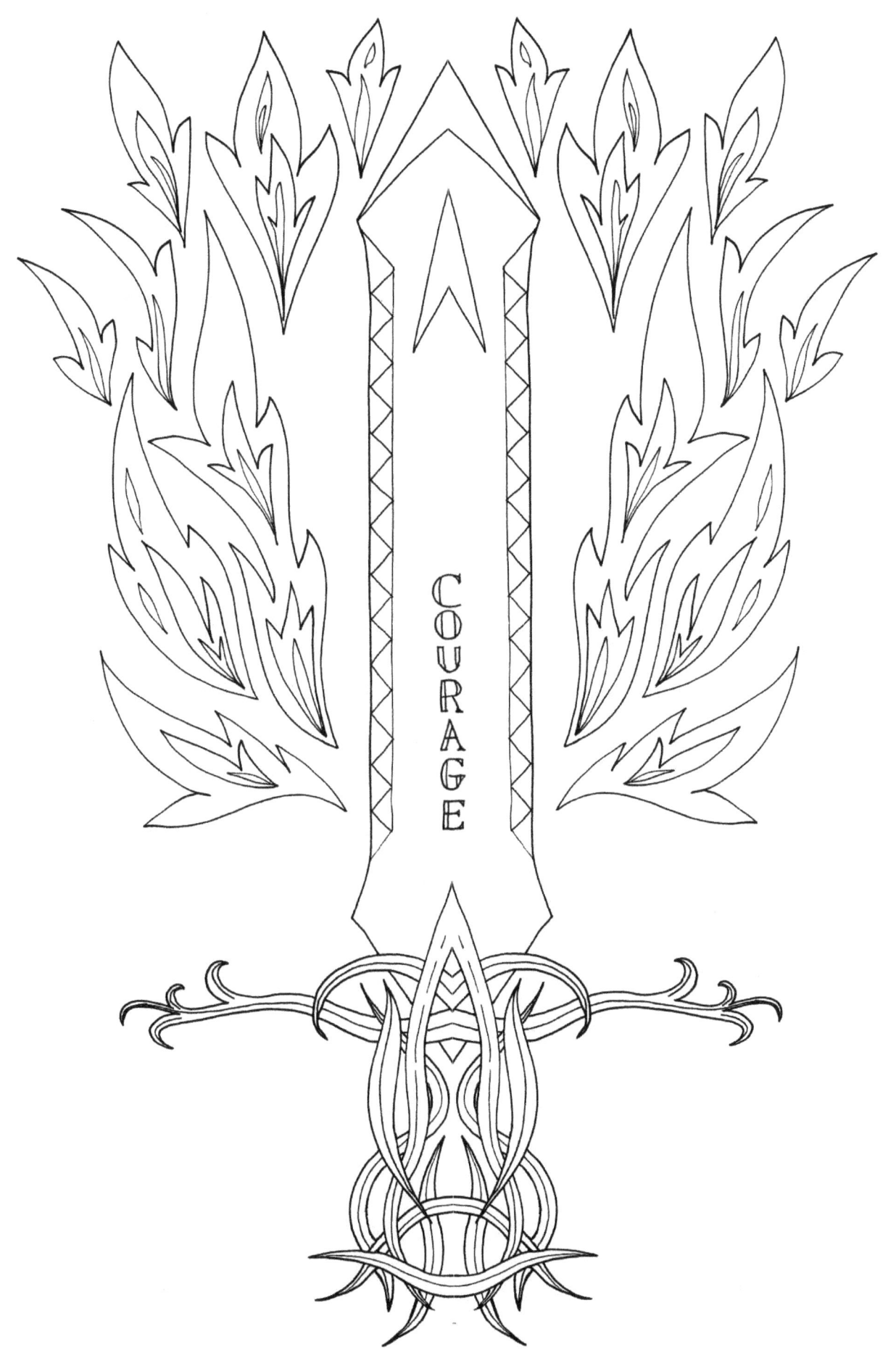

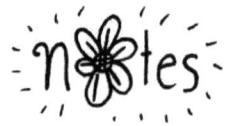

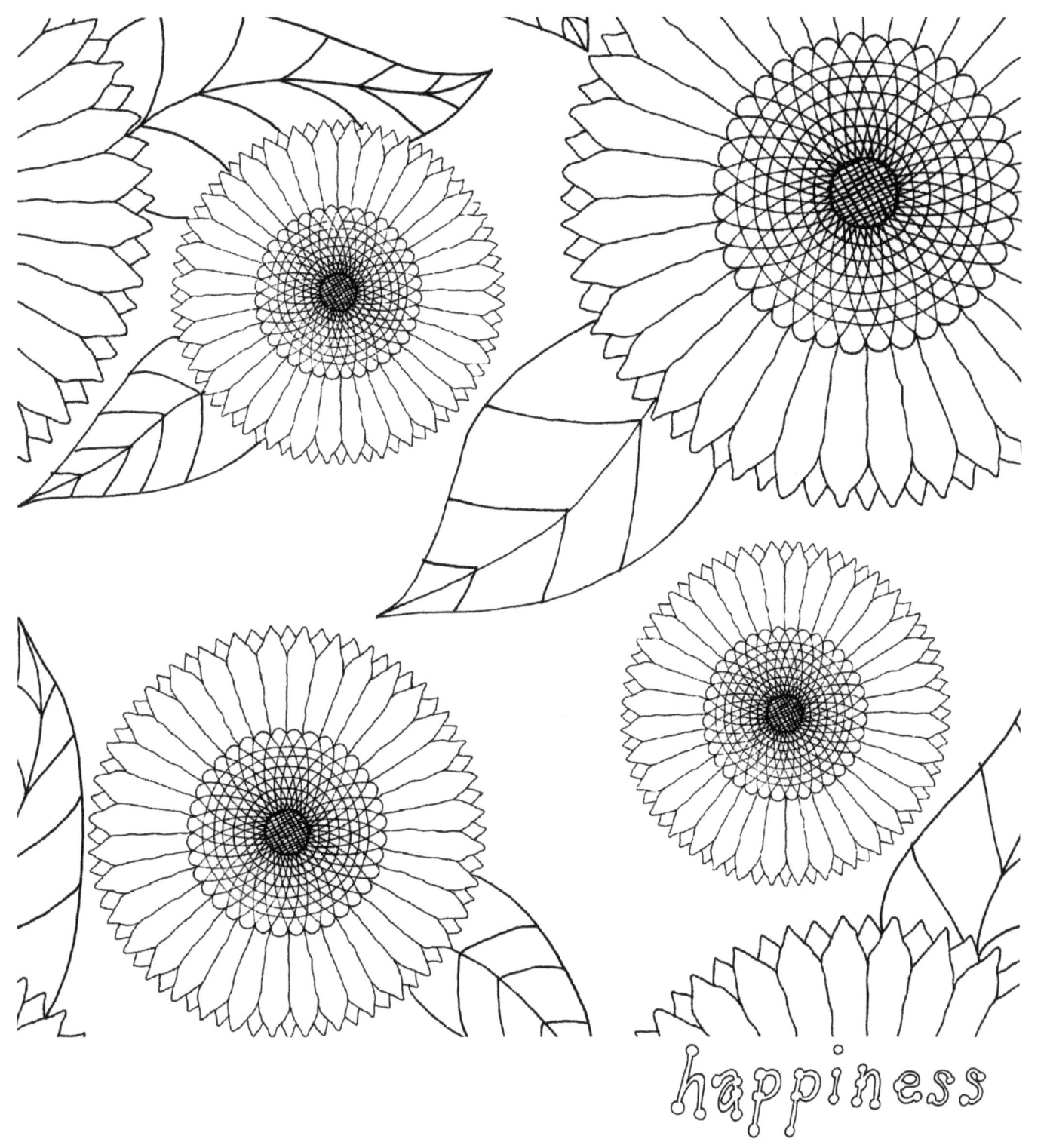

happiness

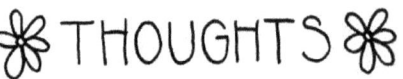

�֎ THOUGHTS ✲

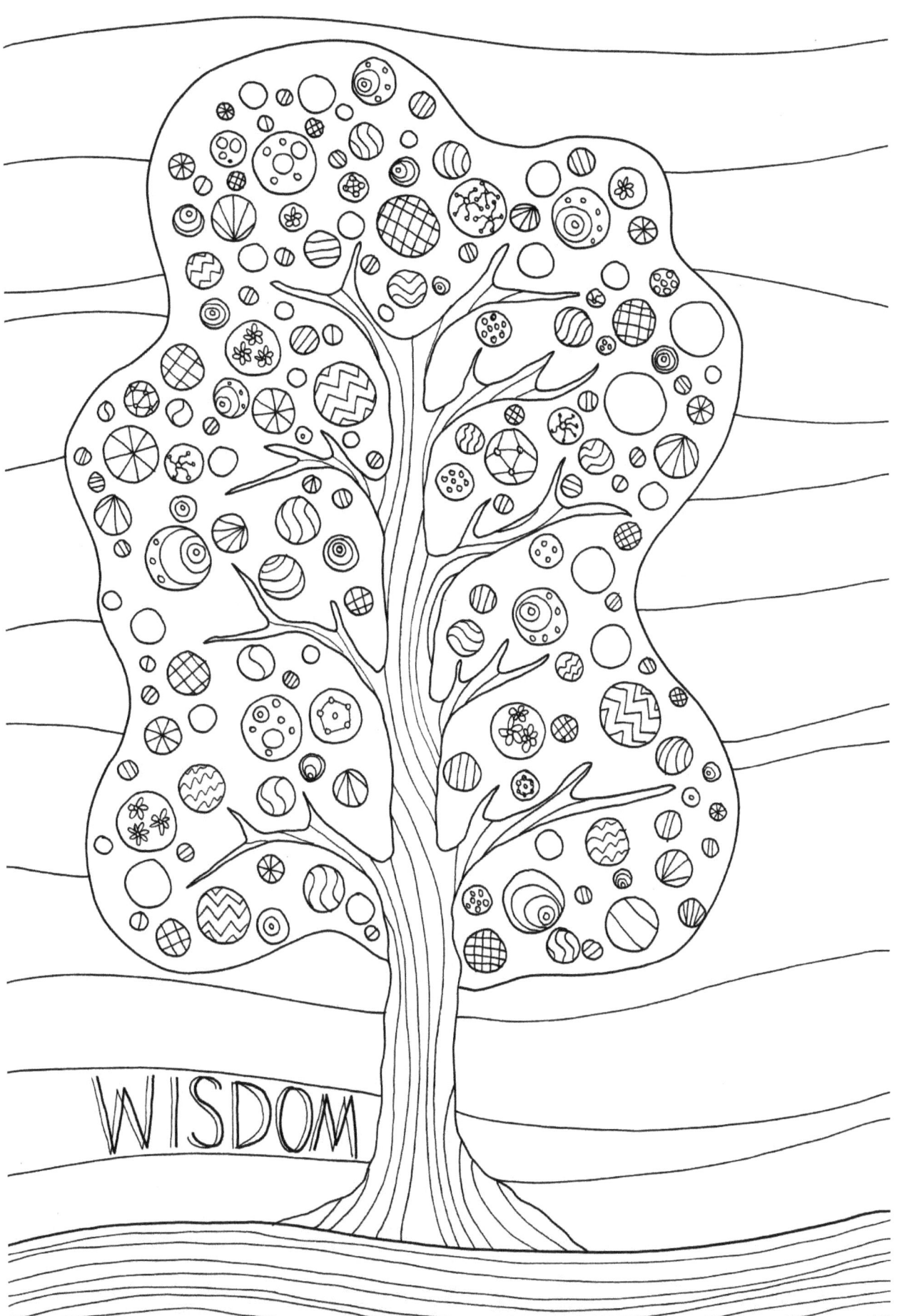

thoughts

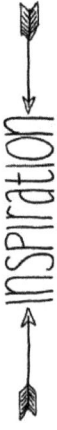

Inspiration

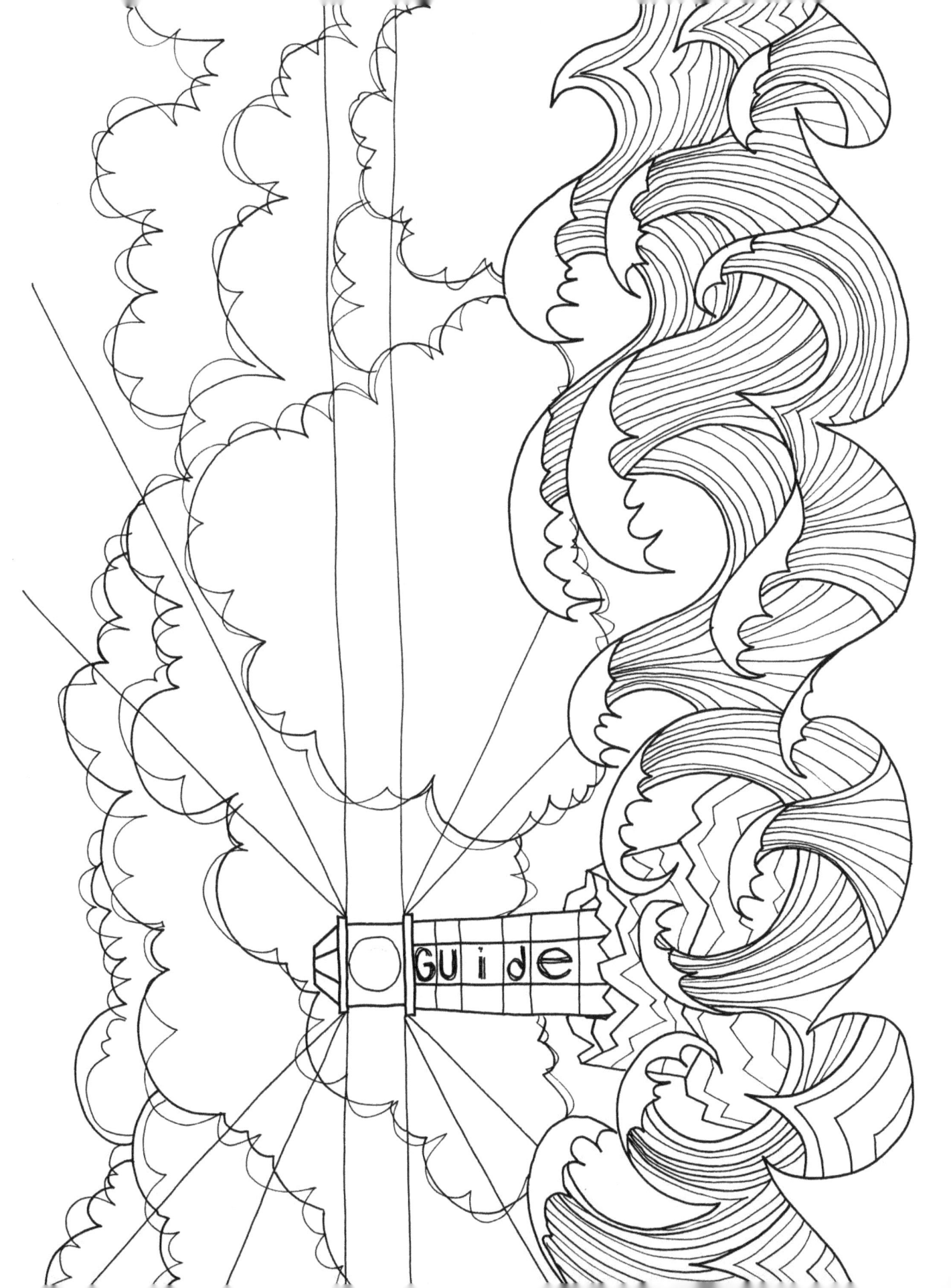

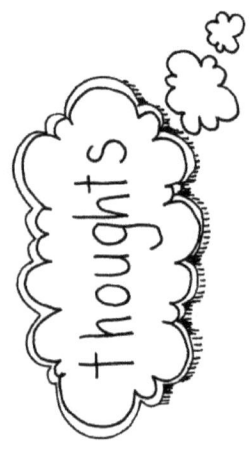

thoughts

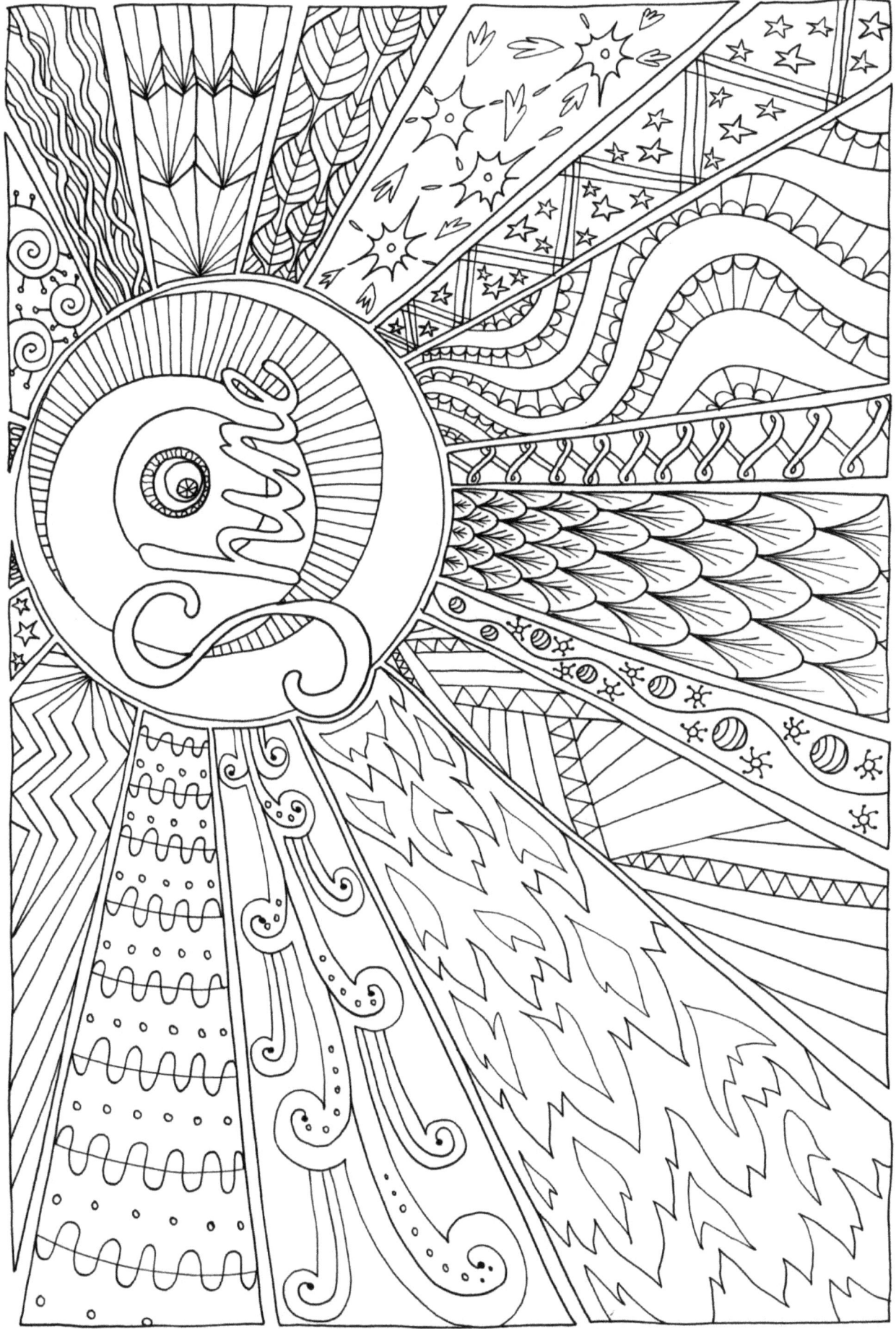

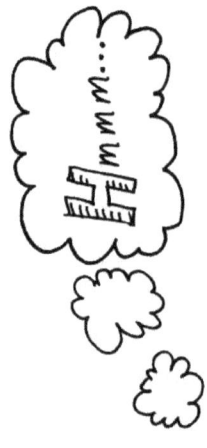

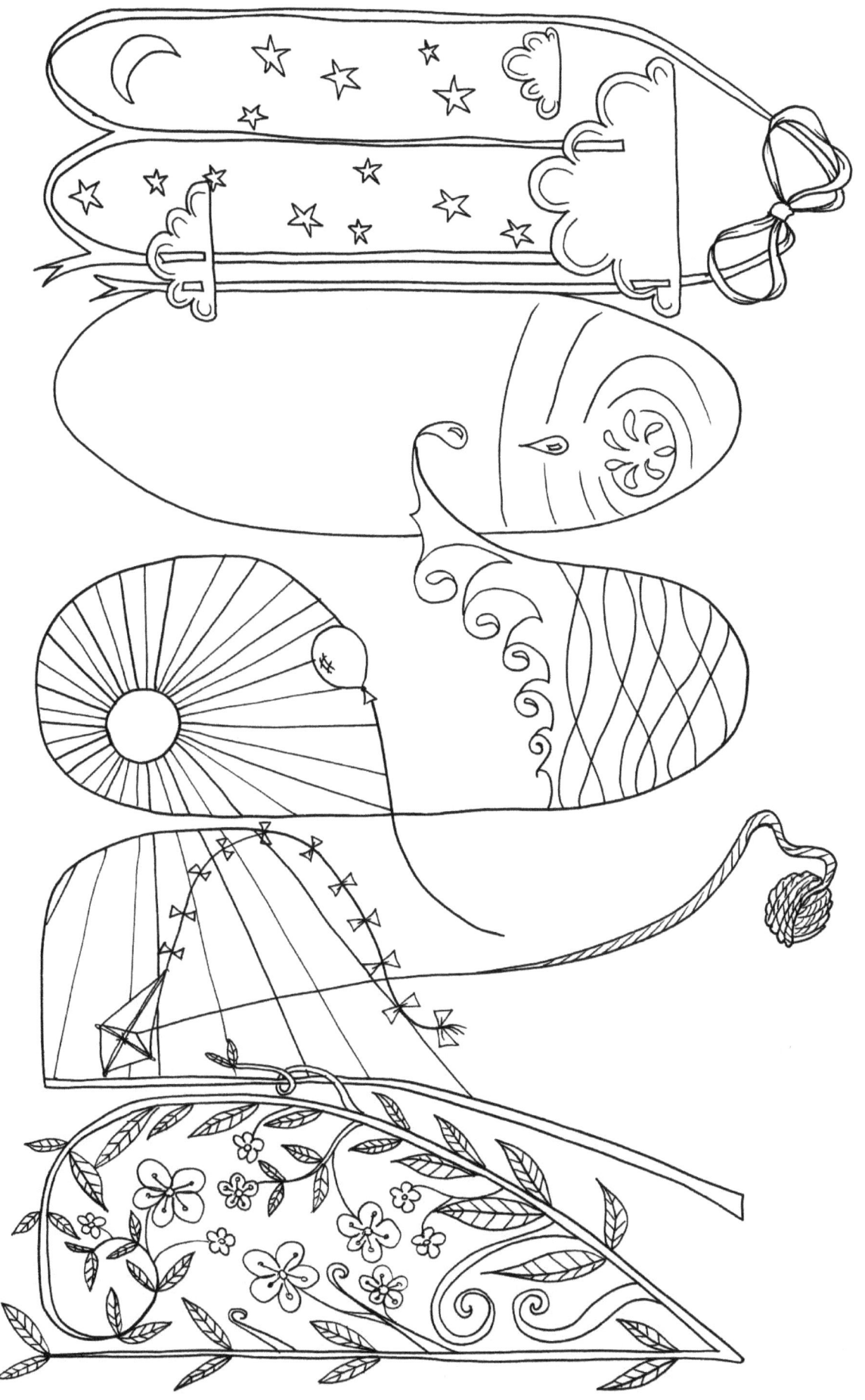

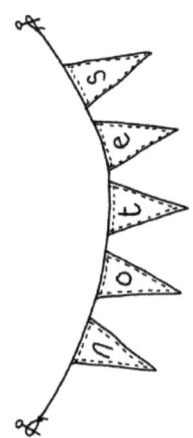

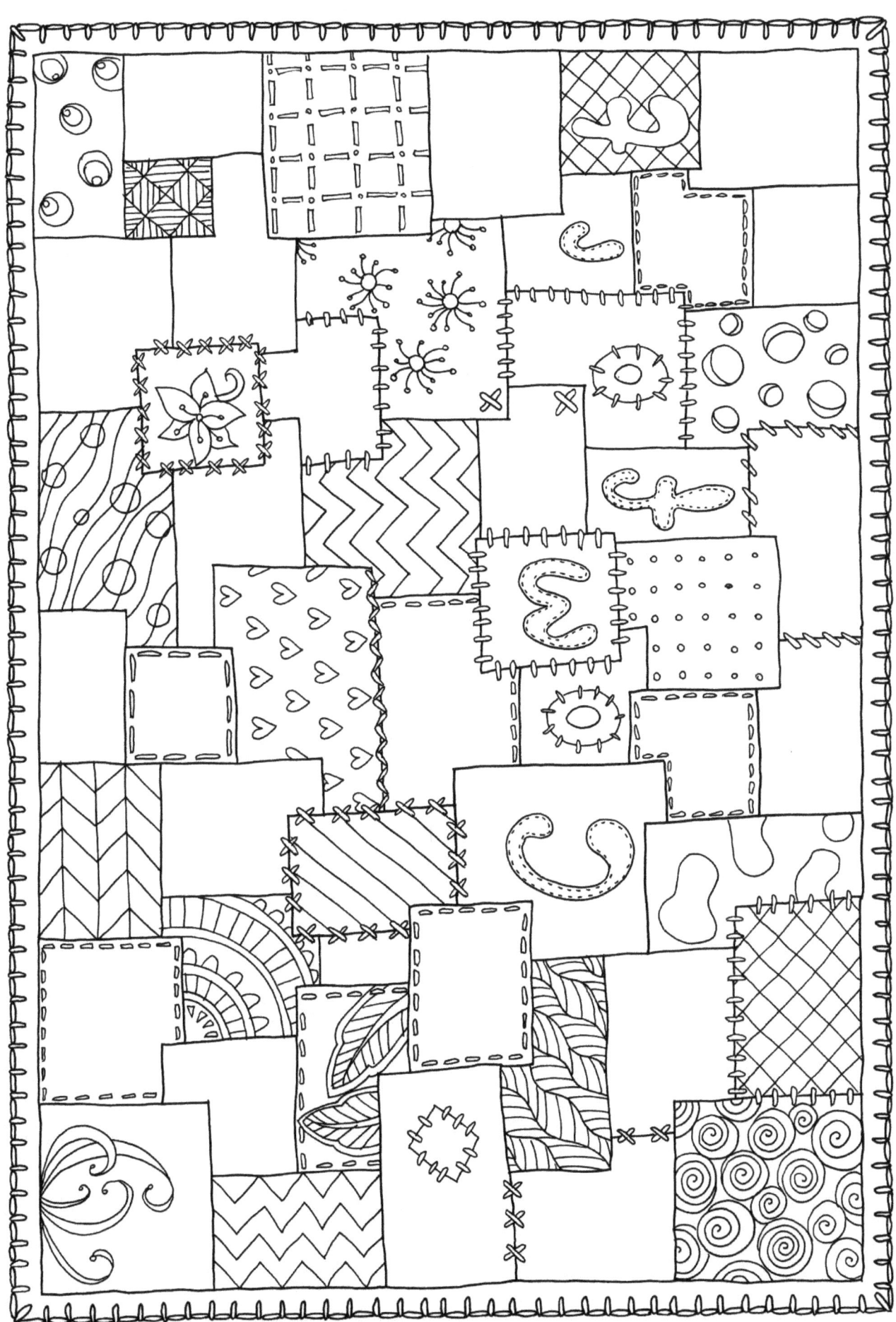

thoughts

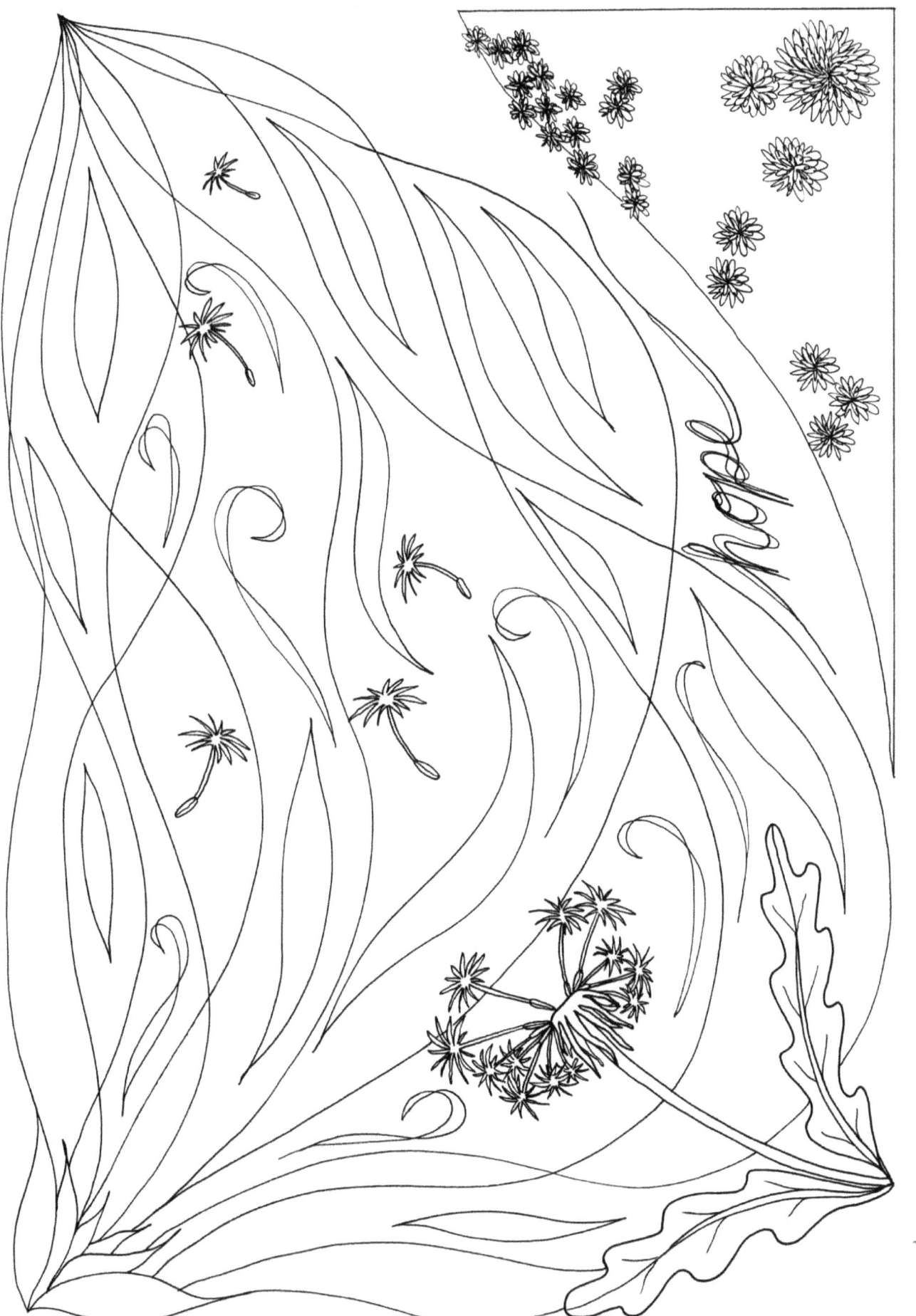

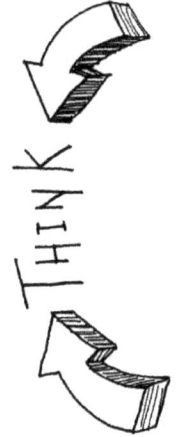

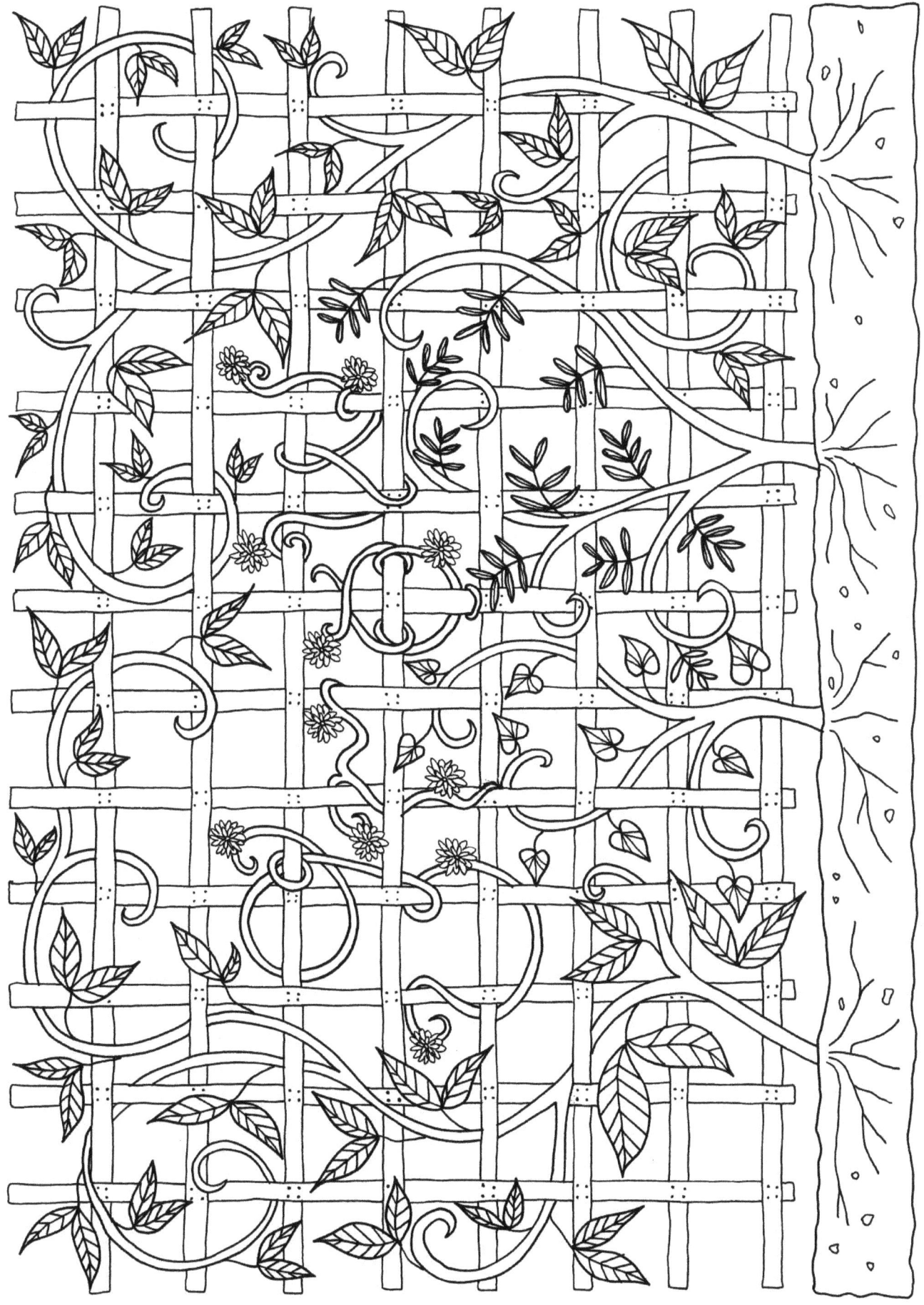

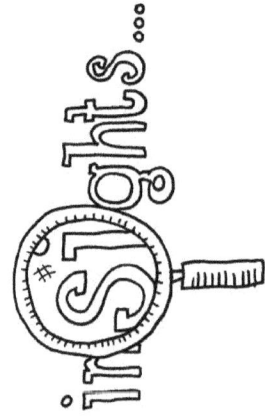
InSights...

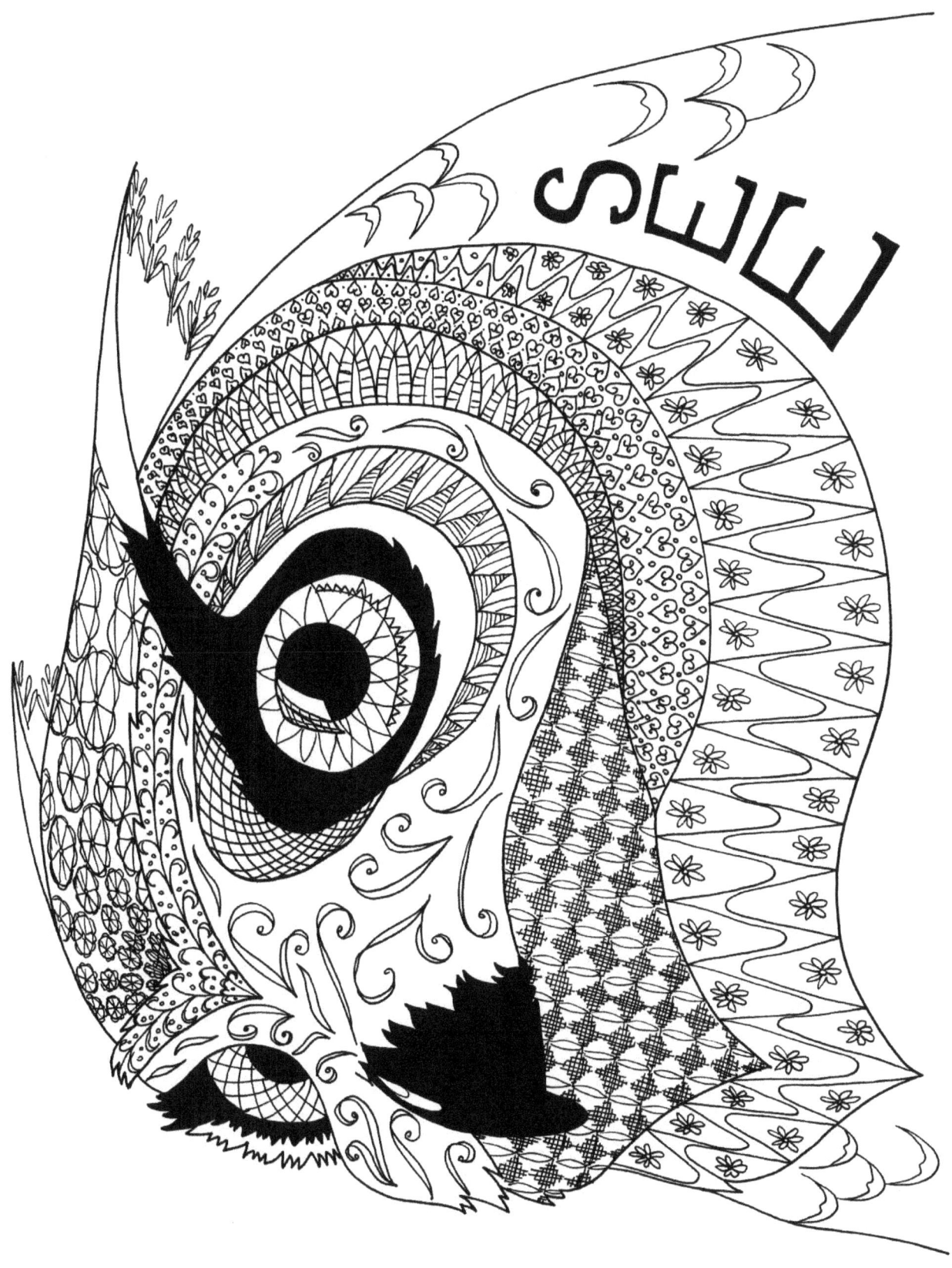

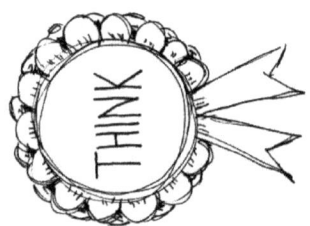

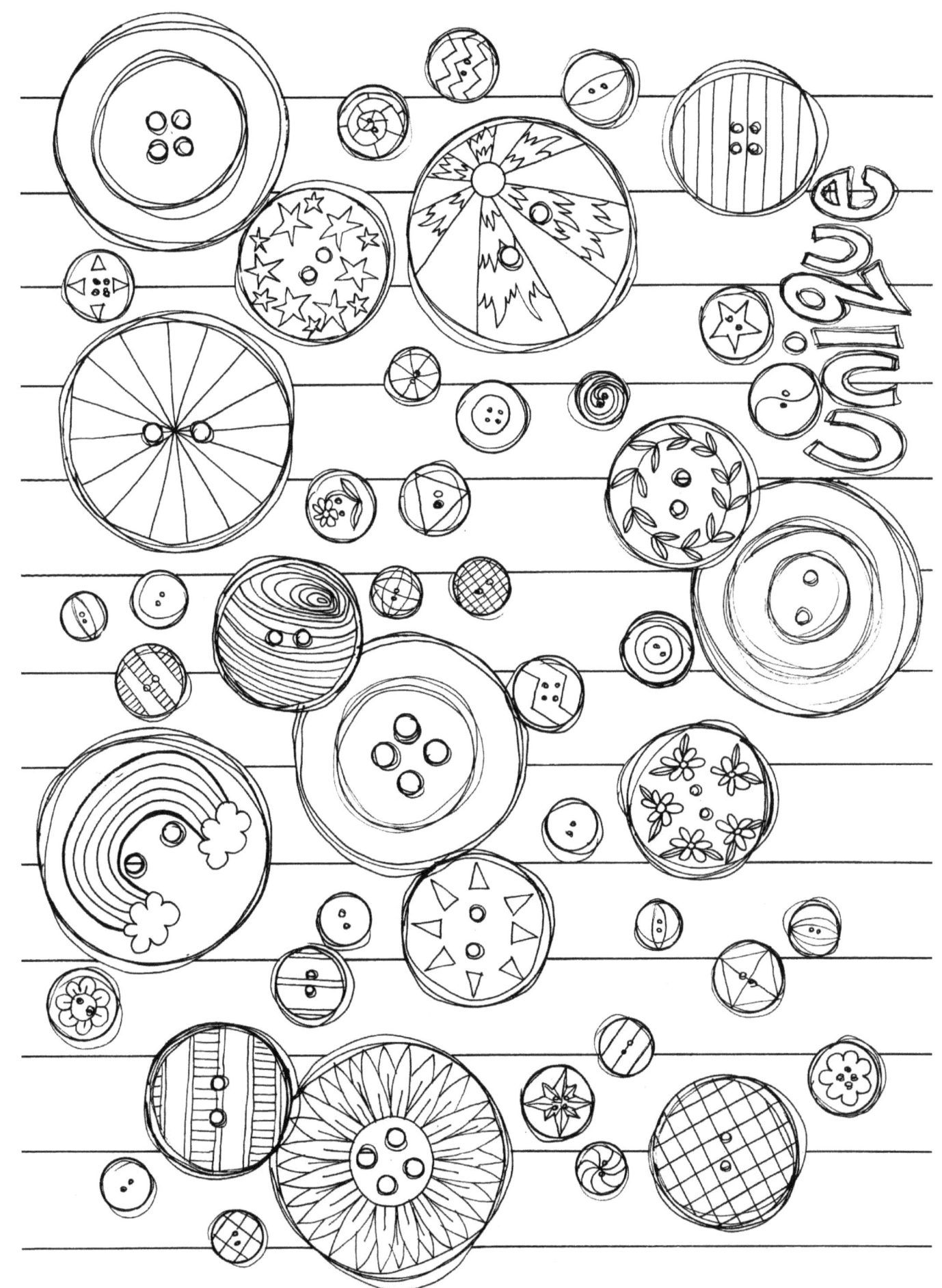

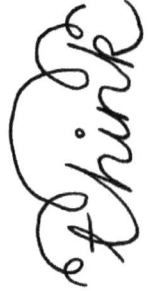

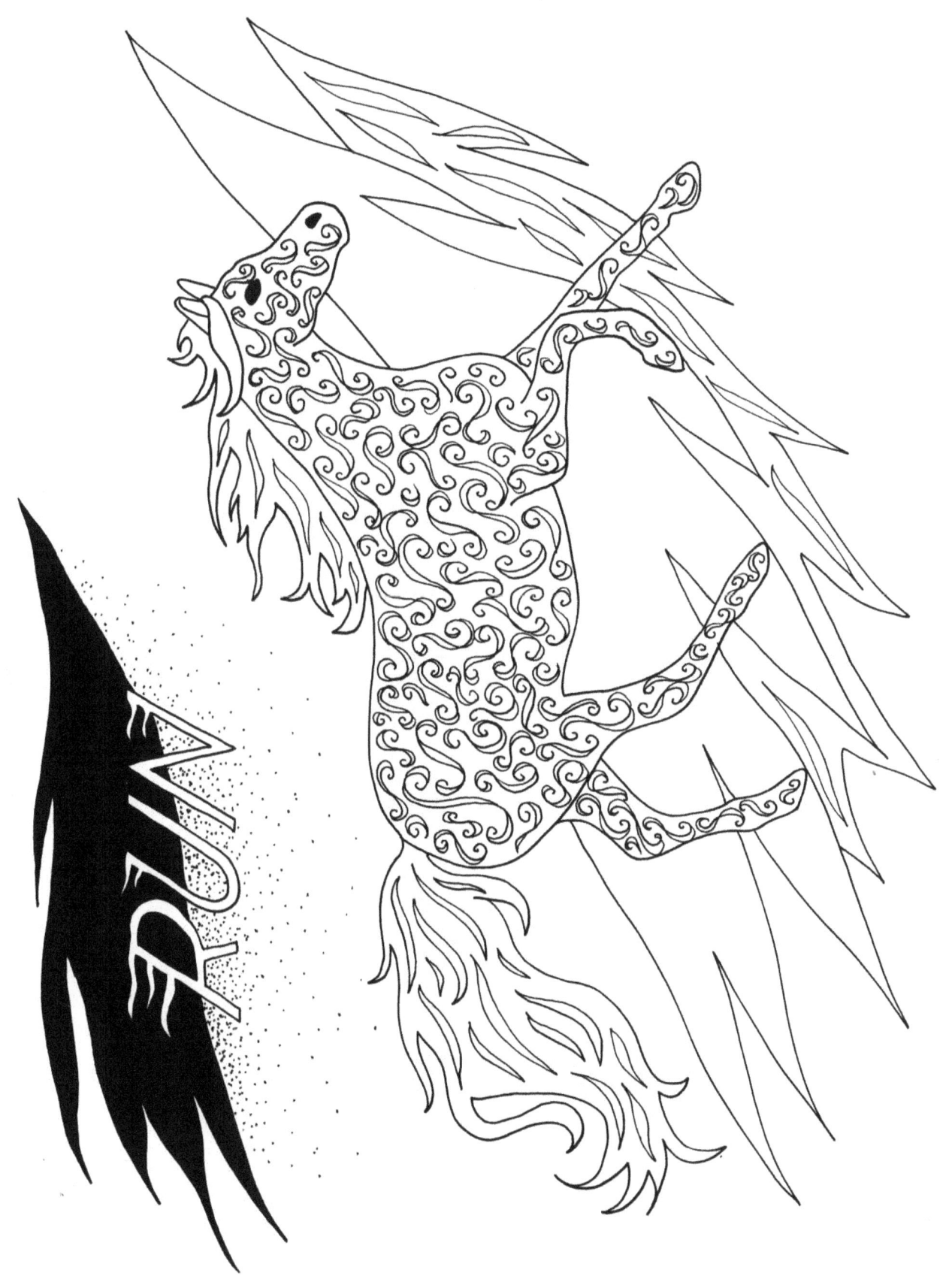

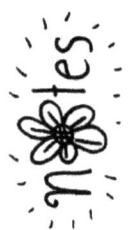

notes

TRANSFORM

TRANSFORM

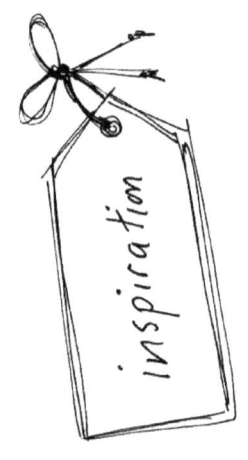

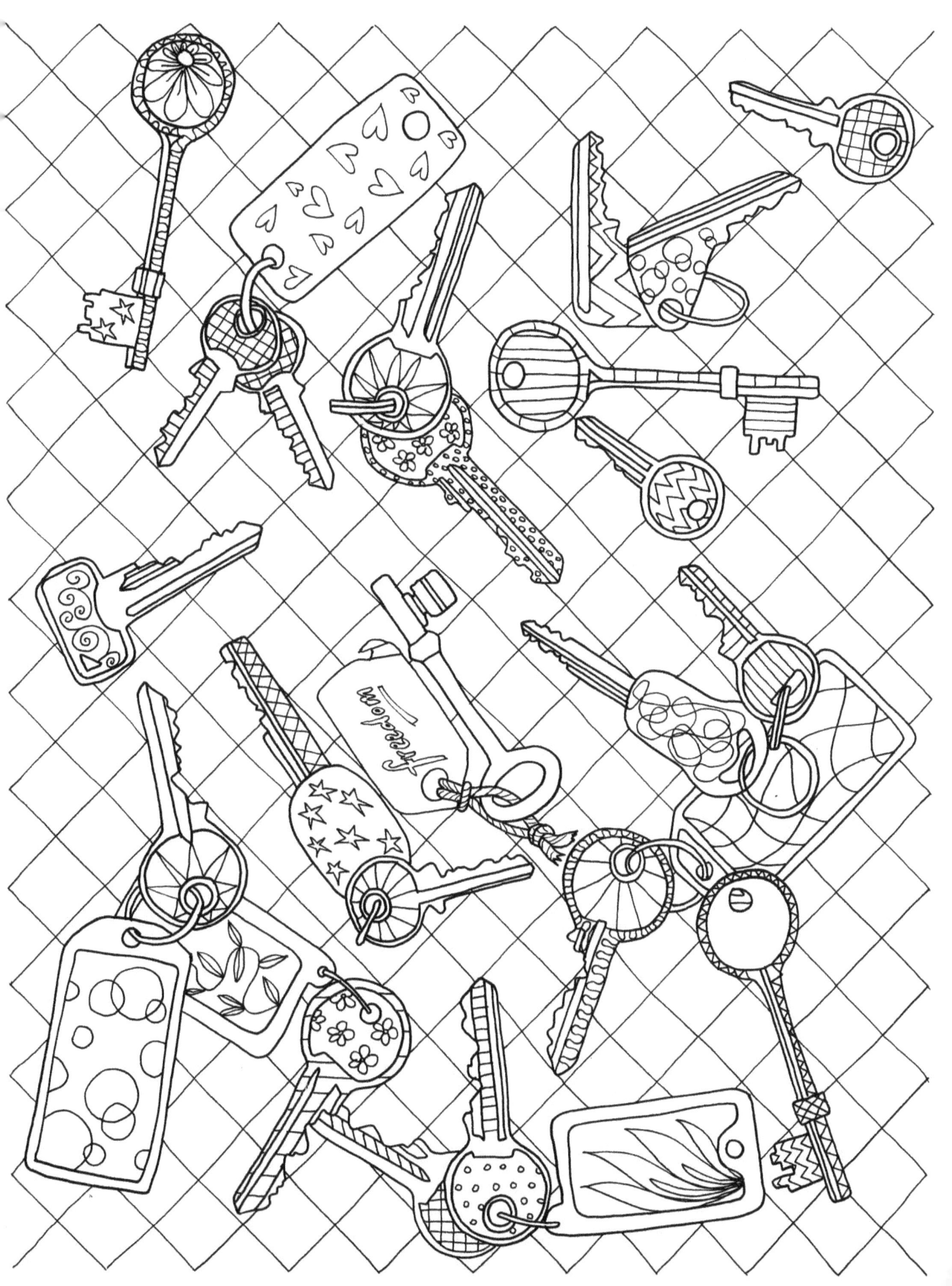

notes

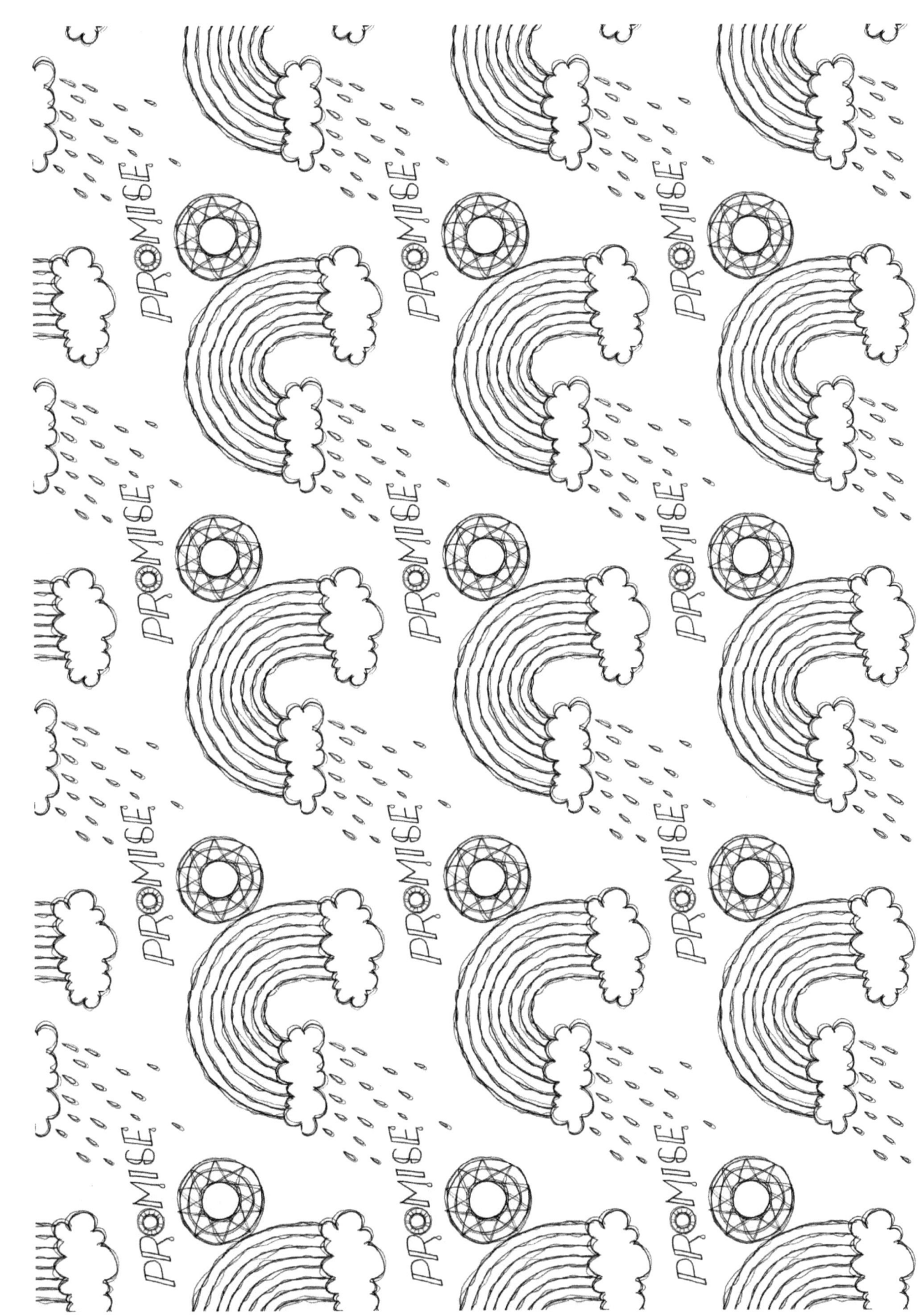

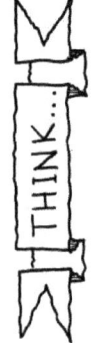

THINK....

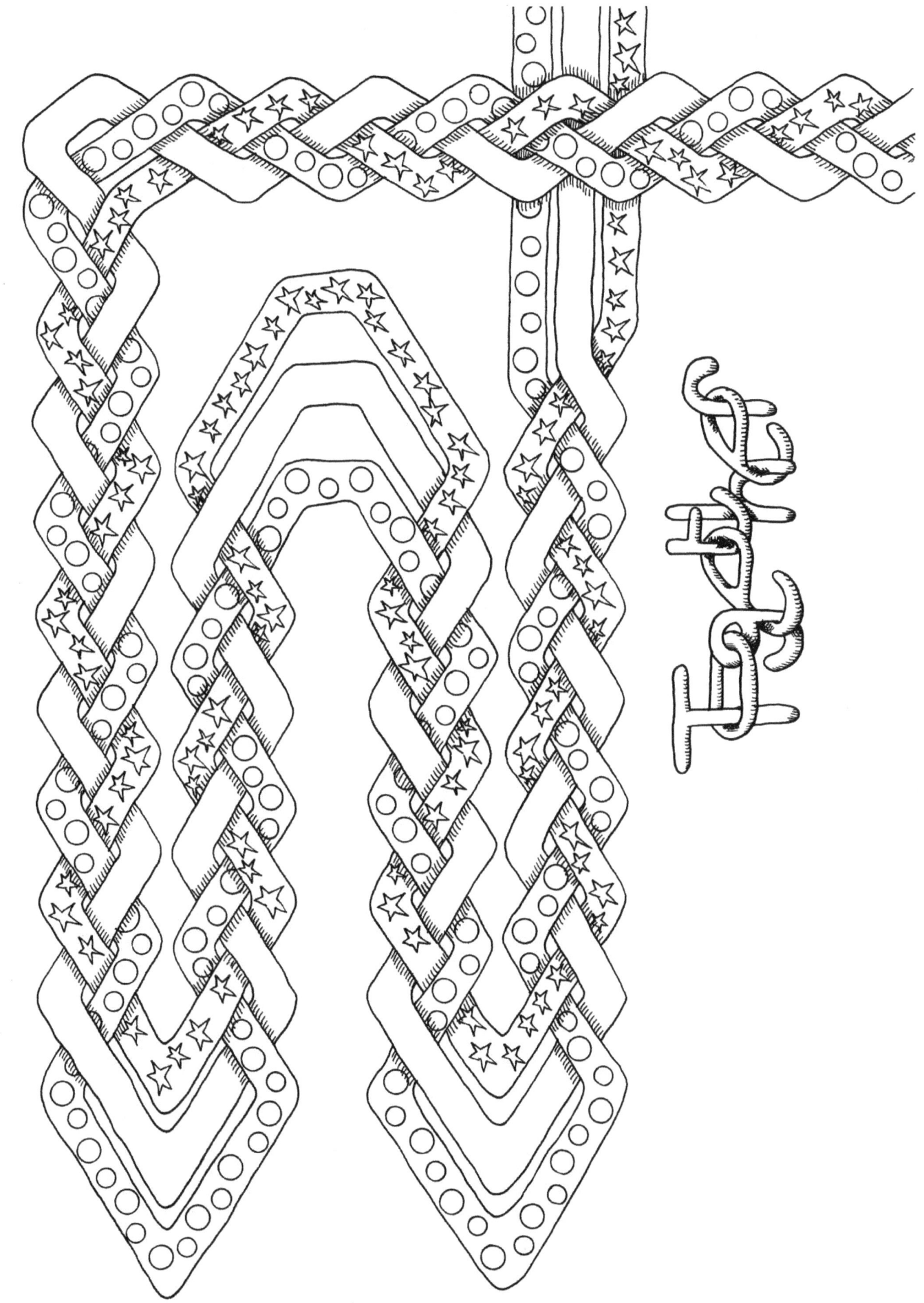

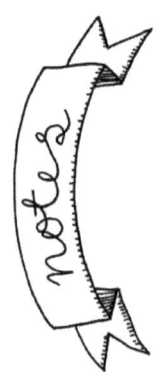

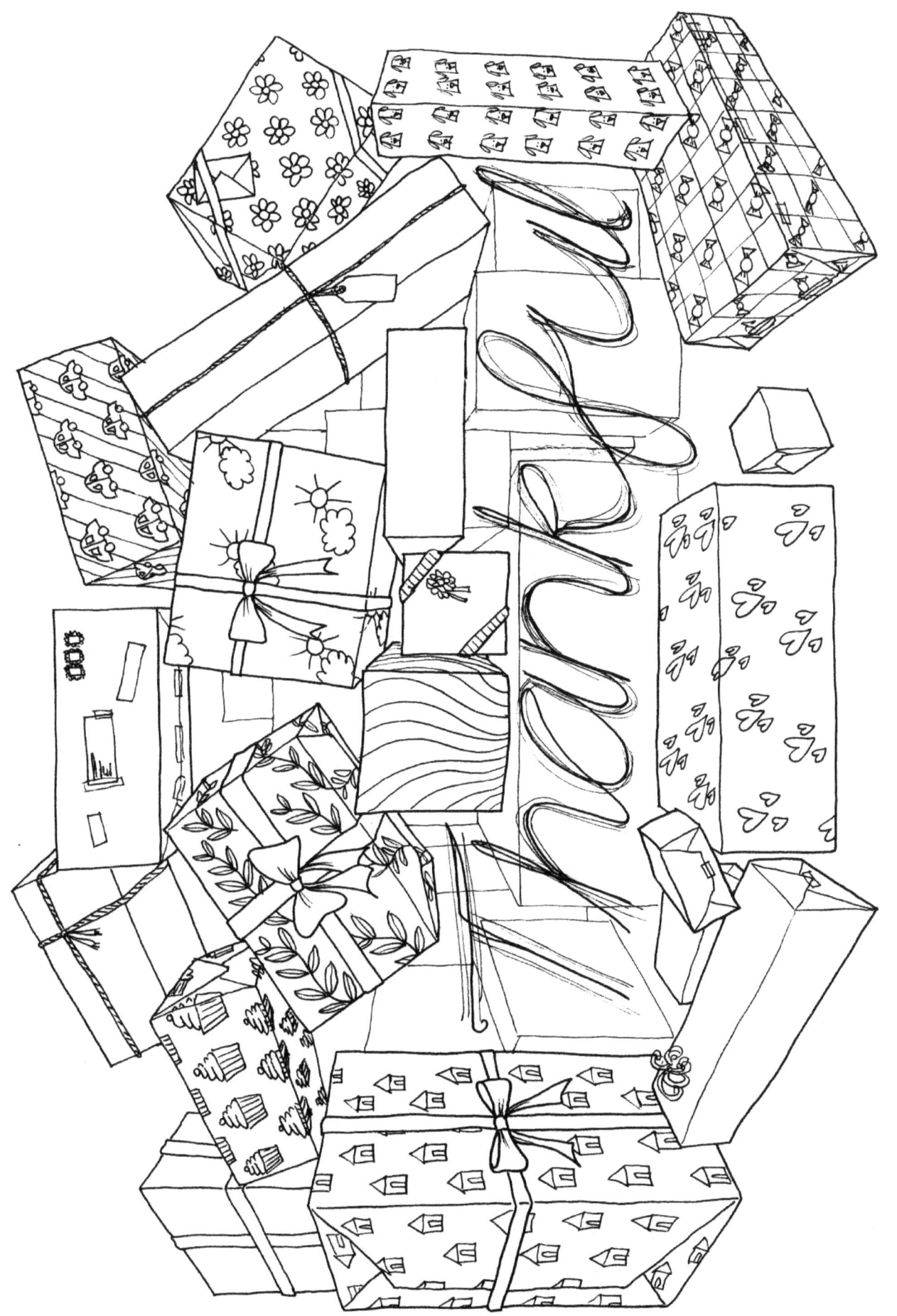

www.ingramcontent.com/pod-product-compliance
Lightning Source LLC
Chambersburg PA
CBHW052144170526
45159CB00018B/3154